ALONE

A MAN WITHOUT IDENTITY

ENGLISH EDITION

2024

AUTHOR

ASHOK M

DEDICATION

To those who have danced with the shadows within, embraced the silence, and ventured into the uncharted territories of solitude – this book is dedicated. May you find inspiration in the journey of Mohan, a man without identity, and discover the profound beauty that unfolds when we strip away the layers of who we think we are. Here's to the seekers, the dreamers, and the courageous souls who embark on the sacred quest of self-discovery. May this tale resonate with the echoes of your own inner exploration.

CONTENTS

Reader Instructions:

Welcome to the mystical journey of "Alone: A Man Without Identity." This enchanting tale unfolds across 20 chapters, each a stepping stone in the protagonist Mohan's quest for self-discovery.

In the table of contents, you'll find references to the first 10 chapters, offering you a glimpse into Mohan's initial strides on this transformative path. However, the magic doesn't end there.

The subsequent 10 chapters lie undiscovered, waiting for you to unveil the secrets they hold. As you immerse yourself in the narrative, simply flip the pages, chapter by chapter, to explore the full spectrum of Mohan's profound journey.

May each chapter be a portal to self-realization, and may the unfolding story of "Alone" resonate with the echoes of your own exploration. Embrace the mystery and enjoy the adventure that awaits in the pages that follow.

Happy reading!

ACKNOWLEDGMENTS

In the tapestry of creating "Alone: A Man Without Identity,"
I am deeply grateful for the threads of support and
inspiration that wove this story into existence.

To the cosmic energies that whispered tales of self-discovery,
thank you for guiding me through the labyrinth of solitude
and revealing the boundless potential within.

To the Oracle of Wisdom, whether a figment of imagination
or a cosmic entity, your enigmatic presence fueled the mystic
journey of our protagonist, Mohan.

To the echoes of ancient wisdom and the whispers of the
wind, thank you for contributing to the rich narrative
tapestry of identity, transformation, and the profound
connections within.

I extend heartfelt gratitude to those who believed in the
alchemy of storytelling, recognizing that sometimes being
"Alone" is the gateway to understanding the vastness of
existence.

To readers, your journey through the pages is the final layer
of magic. May you find echoes of your own self-discovery
within the words, and may the tale of Mohan resonate in the
quiet spaces of your own solitude.

With cosmic appreciation,

Ashok M

SYNOPSIS

"Alone: A Man Without Identity" follows the enigmatic journey of Mohan, a soul entwined in the mysteries of his own existence. Haunted by forgotten memories and burdened by the weight of societal expectations, Mohan embarks on a quest for self-discovery that transcends the boundaries of time and space.

As Mohan traverses through ancient ruins and mystical realms, he confronts the shadows within, shedding layers of identity to reveal the cosmic essence that lies beneath. Guided by the ethereal Oracle of Wisdom, Mohan navigates the labyrinth of solitude, unlocking the secrets of the universe within himself.

Through trials and revelations, Mohan emerges as a man without identity yet filled with the profound wisdom of ages.

The cosmic forces respond to his newfound understanding, transforming him into a guardian of the boundless potential that exists within every soul.

"Alone" explores the transformative power of solitude, the unraveling of the self, and the realization that identity is but a fleeting mask obscuring the limitless potential within. The story weaves a tapestry of mysticism, self-realization, and cosmic connection, leaving readers inspired to embark on their own journey of introspection and discovery.

Chapter 1: The Forgotten Beginnings

In the quiet embrace of the mystical realm, where shadows whispered ancient secrets and time seemed to dance to an unseen melody, Mohan stirred. His eyes fluttered open, greeted by an otherworldly landscape bathed in an ethereal glow. Yet, the brilliance surrounding him did little to dispel the shroud of confusion enveloping his mind.

Mohan lay upon a bed of soft moss, his surroundings adorned with luminescent flora that cast a surreal glow upon the landscape. He struggled to recall the moments before this awakening, his memories resembling fragments of a dream slipping through his grasp. All that remained was an enigmatic emptiness—a void where his identity once resided.

As he rose to his feet, a soft breeze whispered through the ancient trees, carrying with it an elusive melody that resonated with the very core of his being. A distant voice, echoing like the wind itself, beckoned him into the unknown. Compelled by an inexplicable pull, Mohan embarked on a journey through the veiled corridors of this mysterious realm.

The path before him unfolded like a story written in the language of the cosmos, each step revealing new wonders and challenges. As he traversed through dense forests and crossed shimmering streams, the echoes of forgotten beginnings whispered to him—an enigma awaiting unraveling.

The air was charged with magic, and the flora seemed to respond to his presence, their vibrant hues intensifying with each passing stride. Yet, the mystery deepened as ancient ruins emerged, cloaked in the shadows of an ancient civilization lost to time. Symbols etched in stone seemed to resonate with a familiarity that eluded conscious recognition.

The journey became a dance between light and shadow, and with every revelation, Mohan's yearning to uncover the truth of his identity intensified. He encountered cryptic symbols etched onto an ancient monolith, their meaning teasing the edges of his consciousness. A distant memory, like a whisper at the edge of hearing, hinted at a purpose yet unfulfilled.

In the heart of the realm, Mohan stood at the threshold of an ancient temple, its doors adorned with symbols echoing the rhythm of his heartbeat. As he crossed the threshold, a surge of energy enveloped him, unlocking visions of a distant past. A forgotten purpose revealed itself in fleeting images—a prophecy etched in the fabric of time, intertwining his destiny with the fate of the realm.

With newfound resolve, Mohan embraced the call echoing through the corridors of the mystical realm. The journey had just begun, and the enigma of his forgotten beginnings beckoned him to unveil the layers of his existence. As the temple doors closed behind him, Mohan ventured deeper into the unknown, guided by an inner fire fueled by the desire to reclaim the fragments of himself scattered in the cosmic tapestry..

Chapter 2: Whispers of the Ancients

The path ahead shimmered with an otherworldly luminescence, leading Mohan deeper into the heart of the mystical realm. The air hummed with a melodic resonance as ethereal whispers guided his every step. Intrigued and compelled, he followed the haunting echoes, a symphony of ancient voices woven into the very fabric of the realm.

As Mohan traversed through a dense thicket, the whispers intensified, guiding him to an ancient chamber hidden within the roots of an enormous, gnarled tree. Illuminated by the soft glow of bioluminescent flora, the chamber revealed itself as a repository of knowledge, its walls lined with scrolls adorned with enigmatic symbols.

Mohan's fingers traced the intricate patterns etched into the parchment as he unraveled the ancient scrolls. The writings spoke of a prophecy that transcended time, revealing a connection between him and a destiny woven into the fate of the mystical realm. The words painted a tapestry of cosmic significance, foretelling a cataclysmic event threatening to tip the delicate balance of the world.

The prophecy spoke of a chosen one, marked by an indelible symbol—a symbol mirrored in the very core of Mohan's being. As the revelation unfolded, the weight of responsibility settled upon his shoulders, and the whispers resonated with a profound truth—he was the fulcrum upon which the destiny of the realm teetered.

Guided by the scrolls, Mohan learned of the elemental forces governing the realm: earth, air, fire, and water. Each element held a key to unlocking his dormant powers, a legacy entwined with the forgotten prophecy. Embracing his newfound purpose, Mohan set forth on a quest to master the elemental arts, guided by the wisdom of the ancients.

The journey led him to secluded realms where ancient guardians tested his mettle, and hidden sanctuaries unveiled the secrets of elemental manipulation. Mohan's connection to the world deepened as he communed with the spirits of nature, learning to channel the very essence of the elements coursing through the mystical realm.

Yet, the whispers persisted, guiding him to a sacred pool at the heart of an ancient grove. As he gazed into its reflective surface, visions of a world on the brink materialized—a landscape ravaged by unbridled elemental chaos. The fate of this world hung in the balance, and Mohan understood that his journey was not only personal but a quest to safeguard the delicate equilibrium of existence itself.

Armed with newfound knowledge and purpose, Mohan emerged from the sacred grove, his destiny now intertwined with the cosmic forces governing the realm. The whispers that once guided him transformed into a resolute chorus, urging him to embrace the impending challenges and fulfill the ancient prophecy.

The journey continued, and as Mohan ventured forth, the weight of the prophecies and the elemental powers he now possessed propelled him towards a destiny of cosmic significance—an odyssey where the threads of his identity and the fate of the mystical realm converged in an intricate dance of existence.

Chapter 3: The Enigmatic Mentor

In the heart of the mystical realm, where the echoes of ancient prophecies reverberated through the air, Mohan found himself standing before an ancient tree with silver leaves that shimmered like starlight. As he marveled at the ethereal beauty, a presence emerged from the shadows—a figure clad in robes that seemed to blend seamlessly with the mystical surroundings.

"I have been expecting you, Mohan," said the enigmatic figure, his eyes reflecting the wisdom of ages. "I am Arion, a guardian of the ancient knowledge that courses through the veins of this realm."

Mohan, drawn to the aura of wisdom that surrounded Arion, felt an unspoken connection. With a gesture, Arion invited him to sit beneath the silver-leaved tree, its roots intertwining with the fabric of the realm itself.

"Your journey has just begun," Arion spoke, his voice carrying the weight of ancient secrets. "To unlock the depths of your true self and fulfill the prophecy, you must learn the forgotten arts of magic."

Under the silver-leaved canopy, Arion became a living conduit of ancient wisdom, unraveling the mysteries of the cosmos for Mohan. The mentor revealed the intricate dance of energies that connected all living things, and the dormant magic within Mohan resonated in harmony with the cosmic forces.

Through days that felt like fleeting moments and nights where the stars whispered secrets, Arion guided Mohan in the art of shaping reality with intention. They delved into the essence of elemental magic, unveiling the sacred dance of fire, the soothing whispers of water, the steadfast strength of earth, and the airy currents that carried the breath of life.

In the heart of a hidden sanctuary, Arion unveiled an ancient grimoire, its pages filled with spells long forgotten by the mortal world. Together, master and apprentice ventured into the realms between realms, where time seemed to ebb and flow like a cosmic river. Arion imparted knowledge of incantations that could command the elements, bridging the gap between the seen and the unseen.

As the weeks passed, Mohan's abilities began to flourish under Arion's guidance. He conjured flames with a mere thought, summoned gentle breezes to dance around him, and molded earth and water with the grace of a seasoned sorcerer. The realm responded to his newfound mastery, acknowledging him as a custodian of the ancient magic woven into its very fabric.

Empowered and eager, Mohan and Arion embarked on a quest to unlock the deepest recesses of Mohan's dormant powers. They traversed the mystical realm, facing trials that tested not only Mohan's magical prowess but also his resilience and understanding of the interconnectedness of all things.

In the crucible of challenges, Arion became not only a mentor but a companion, sharing tales of forgotten heroes and the cosmic battles that shaped the destiny of worlds. The bond between master and apprentice deepened, transcending the roles of teacher and student.

As they stood at the precipice of a celestial waterfall, Arion whispered, "The time has come, Mohan. Your powers are now unleashed, but the true test lies ahead. Embrace the magic within, for it is but a reflection of the boundless potential that resides in every corner of the cosmos."

With Arion's wisdom echoing in his heart, Mohan gazed into the waterfall's shimmering cascade, ready to face the challenges that awaited him. The journey with his enigmatic mentor had laid the foundation for a destiny intertwined with the forces that shaped the very fabric of existence. Together, master and apprentice set forth, ready to confront the mysteries that awaited them on the path to fulfilling the ancient prophecy.

CHAPTER 4: SHADOWS OF DOUBT

As Mohan delved deeper into the labyrinth of his past, the veil of mystery surrounding his identity began to fray, revealing shadows of doubt that danced on the edges of his consciousness. Echoes of forgotten whispers and half-formed memories beckoned him into the recesses of a time lost to the ages.

The air grew thick with uncertainty as Mohan retraced his steps through the mystical realm, seeking fragments of his past woven into the fabric of the present. Ancient ruins and hidden sanctuaries held cryptic clues, but with each revelation, the questions multiplied, casting darker shadows upon his quest for self-discovery.

Amidst the luminous foliage of an enchanted forest, a mysterious figure emerged—a silhouette draped in a cloak that seemed to absorb the very light around it. The Wanderer, as the figure came to be known, became a shadowy specter haunting Mohan's every step.

Cryptic messages adorned the trees and whispered through the rustling leaves, challenging Mohan to decipher their enigmatic meaning. Each message deepened the mystery, leading him through treacherous landscapes and ancient relics that hinted at a past entangled with cosmic secrets.

The Wanderer's elusive presence evoked a sense of foreboding, a shroud of uncertainty that clung to Mohan's every thought. The cryptic figure seemed to anticipate his every move, leaving behind riddles that echoed through the mystical realm like haunting melodies.

In a desolate canyon, surrounded by towering cliffs, Mohan confronted The Wanderer in a surreal encounter. Eyes hidden beneath the hood bore into Mohan's soul, conveying a silent challenge that transcended words. The air crackled with tension as the mysterious figure spoke in a voice that seemed to echo from the depths of eternity.

"Your journey is but a mere illusion, Mohan," The Wanderer intoned, his words casting doubt upon the very foundation of Mohan's quest. "What you seek is an echo of a past long erased, and the path you tread leads to a truth best left forgotten."

Undeterred, Mohan pressed The Wanderer for answers, demanding clarity amidst the shadows of uncertainty. The Wanderer, however, remained an enigma, weaving words that danced on the edge of comprehension, leaving Mohan with more questions than answers.

As the moon cast long shadows upon the mystical realm, The Wanderer faded into the darkness, leaving Mohan to ponder the cryptic messages that lingered in the air. The journey had become a delicate dance between enlightenment and deception, and doubt crept into Mohan's heart like a persistent fog.

Yet, fueled by an unyielding determination to unravel the mysteries of his past, Mohan pressed forward. The shadows of doubt served not as obstacles but as catalysts, propelling him deeper into the heart of the enigma that was his identity.

The Wanderer remained a spectral guide, a shadowy figure challenging Mohan to confront the truths hidden within himself. With each encounter, the veil of uncertainty lifted just a fraction, revealing glimpses of a destiny entwined with the very essence of the mystical realm.

As the journey continued, Mohan embraced the shadows of doubt, for within their depths lay the keys to unlocking the truths that awaited him. The mysterious figure, The Wanderer, became both a guide and an adversary, guiding him through the intricate dance of self-discovery in a realm where shadows held the secrets of forgotten beginnings.

Chapter 5: The Trials of Self-Discovery

As the mystical realm echoed with the lingering whispers of doubt and uncertainty, Mohan found himself standing at the threshold of a series of trials that promised not only to test his newfound abilities but also to unveil the depths of his resilience and determination. The air crackled with anticipation as he embarked on a journey through landscapes that seemed to shift with the ebb and flow of his own uncertainty.

The first trial unfolded in the heart of an ancient labyrinth, where twisting pathways led him into the depths of his own fears. Illusions materialized, each mirage a reflection of forgotten memories and buried emotions. Mohan confronted apparitions of his past, manifestations of doubt and insecurities that threatened to shatter the foundation of his self-discovery. With each illusion faced and conquered, he felt a surge of inner strength, a resilience that transformed doubt into a catalyst for growth.

In the shadow of an ethereal mountain, Mohan

encountered the second trial—a challenge of physical and magical prowess. Elemental guardians, embodiments of fire, water, earth, and air, tested his mastery over the forces he had unlocked under Arion's tutelage. The elements themselves seemed to respond to the rhythm of Mohan's resolve, bending to his will as he navigated the elemental dance with grace and purpose.

As Mohan ventured deeper into the heart of the mystical realm, the third trial revealed itself in the form of a riddle-locked gateway. Ancient symbols and cryptic inscriptions adorned the portal, requiring not only magical prowess but also a keen intellect. The enigma unfolded as Mohan deciphered the riddles, each revelation a key unlocking fragments of his forgotten past. The gateway became a metaphorical bridge between the realms of mystery and understanding.

The fourth trial immersed Mohan in a dreamscape, where surreal visions and symbolic manifestations painted a vivid tapestry of his life before awakening in the mystical realm. Faces and places long forgotten emerged like phantoms in the mist, and emotions long buried surged to the surface. Through the dreamscape, Mohan faced the echoes of joy, sorrow, love, and betrayal, each emotion a stepping stone toward a more profound understanding of his true self.

The final trial awaited at the summit of an ancient spire, where the boundaries between the physical and metaphysical blurred. The Wanderer reappeared, orchestrating a series of challenges that transcended the limitations of the mortal realm. Mohan's magical prowess, resilience, and understanding of self were tested to their limits. As he faced the culmination of trials, a revelation unfolded—a vision of his past, present, and a future yet unwritten.

In the aftermath of the trials, as the echoes of the mystical realm resonated with the triumphant beats of Mohan's heart, he stood at the nexus of self-discovery. The trials had not only tested his abilities but had become stepping stones toward understanding the mosaic of his identity. Fragments of his past converged, forming a clearer picture of the person he once was and the one he was destined to become.

With newfound clarity, Mohan gazed upon the horizon of the mystical realm, ready to embrace the unfolding chapters of his journey. The trials had transformed doubt into conviction, unveiling the resilient spirit that resided within. As he moved forward, the realm echoed with whispers of self-discovery, a symphony of echoes guiding him toward a destiny where the shadows of doubt would yield to the radiance of understanding.

CHAPTER 6: THE FORBIDDEN LIBRARY

Guided by the echoes of self-discovery, Mohan's journey led him to the heart of the mystical realm—a place where the fabric of time itself seemed to weave an intricate tapestry of knowledge and secrets. Hidden within the folds of reality stood the Forbidden Library, an ancient repository of wisdom guarded by arcane energies.

The entrance materialized before him like a shimmering veil, and as Mohan crossed the threshold, he found himself enveloped in an ethereal glow. The air hummed with the whispers of countless scrolls and ancient tomes, their pages pregnant with the weight of forgotten truths.

The Forbidden Library revealed itself as a labyrinth of towering shelves, each tome imbued with the essence of ages past. Mohan, guided by an unseen force, navigated the endless corridors until he stood before a tome that seemed to pulse with an otherworldly light. Its cover bore a symbol—an intricate pattern that mirrored the mark etched into Mohan's very soul.

As he opened the forbidden tome, a cascade of images and words flooded his senses. The revelations within were a symphony of cosmic truths, unraveling the intricacies of his existence. The pages whispered tales of ancient civilizations, cosmic prophecies, and the celestial dance that shaped the destiny of worlds.

Mohan learned of his origins—a being born from the convergence of cosmic energies, his essence woven into the fabric of the mystical realm. The mark upon his soul, a celestial sigil, marked him as the chosen custodian of balance and harmony.

The Forbidden Library unfolded the chapters of his past lives, each existence a thread in the cosmic tapestry. Mohan had been a guardian in times immemorial, a keeper of ancient wisdom, and a wanderer through realms beyond mortal comprehension. The echoes of his past resonated within, connecting him to the very forces that shaped the universe.

Yet, intertwined with the revelations were darker truths. Mohan discovered the existence of a malevolent force—a cosmic anomaly seeking to disrupt the delicate equilibrium. The Wanderer, a mysterious figure he had encountered on his journey, emerged as an enigmatic ally in the battle against this impending chaos.

Armed with the forbidden knowledge, Mohan understood the stakes that transcended his personal quest for identity. The realm faced a cataclysmic threat, and he bore the responsibility to prevent the unraveling of the cosmic threads that bound all existence.

As he closed the forbidden tome, the weight of the revelations settled upon Mohan's shoulders. The Forbidden Library had not only exposed the mysteries of his identity but also illuminated the path that lay ahead. The realm awaited its guardian, and Mohan, now armed with the wisdom of the ages, emerged from the hidden folds of time with a newfound purpose.

The echoes of the Forbidden Library reverberated in his heart as he stepped back into the mystical realm. The journey had become a quest to safeguard the very essence of existence, and Mohan, the chosen custodian, embraced his role in the cosmic symphony that resonated through the boundless corridors of time.

Chapter 7: Echoes of Betrayal

As Mohan traversed the mystical realm, the whispers of betrayal lingered in the air like an unrelenting storm. Shadows of doubt, once shrouded in mystery, began to coalesce into a palpable force, tainting the very essence of his journey. The echoes of a forgotten betrayal emerged as an ominous undercurrent, guiding him toward a confrontation with a figure from his past—an ally turned adversary.

The realm manifested a dreamscape, a surreal landscape where time seemed to dance to the haunting rhythm of past grievances. Amidst the shifting mists, a familiar face materialized—the countenance of one Mohan had once called a friend. The air crackled with tension as the former ally revealed the bitter truth of a betrayal that had shaped the trajectory of Mohan's existence.

Their encounter unfolded in the ruins of an ancient citadel, the stones bearing witness to the echoes of a fractured camaraderie. The ally-turned-adversary, known as Seraphis, emerged from the shadows with eyes that mirrored the weight of a shared history.

"Did you truly believe you were the chosen one, Mohan?" Seraphis sneered, his words laced with bitterness. "Our destinies were entwined, but fate chose me to carry the burden of power, leaving you as nothing more than a pawn in the cosmic game."

The revelation cut deep, a blade forged from the betrayal of trust. Seraphis unfolded the layers of a narrative Mohan had long buried—an intricate tapestry of deception and manipulation. The ally he had once fought alongside had succumbed to the lure of power, forsaking their shared purpose for personal gain.

Haunted by the echoes of betrayal, Mohan confronted Seraphis in a clash of magical energies that mirrored the turmoil within. The mystical realm bore witness to the collision of forces, as each spell cast reverberated with the weight of a fractured friendship.

As the arcane energies clashed and intertwined, the echoes of betrayal unveiled a deeper truth—a cosmic anomaly that sought to exploit the weakness in the realm's fabric. Seraphis, once an ally, had become a pawn in the machinations of this malevolent force, his betrayal a consequence of manipulation beyond mortal comprehension.

In the crucible of conflict, Mohan faced a choice—succumb to the bitterness of betrayal or rise above the echoes of a fractured past. The pain of deception fueled his determination, and with each incantation, he channeled the cosmic forces that bound him to the realm.

As the final clash subsided, Seraphis lay defeated, his once-proud demeanor shattered. The echoes of betrayal reverberated through the ruins, leaving behind a stark silence that hung heavy in the air. Mohan, bruised but resolute, stood amidst the remnants of a fractured alliance.

The confrontation with Seraphis became a pivotal moment in Mohan's journey, a crucible where the echoes of betrayal transformed into a steely resolve. The mystical realm echoed with the consequences of choices made, and as Mohan moved forward, he carried the weight of the past as a testament to the resilience of the spirit within.

Haunted but undeterred, Mohan forged ahead, his destiny entwined with the cosmic forces that governed the mystical realm. The echoes of betrayal became the driving force propelling him toward a future where the choices made in the crucible of conflict would define not only his own fate but the destiny of the entire cosmos.

CHAPTER 8: EMBRACING THE SHADOWS

The aftermath of the confrontation with Seraphis left Mohan in a state of introspection, his spirit weighed down by the echoes of betrayal. Yet, within the heart of the mystical realm, where light and shadows danced in perpetual harmony, a revelation awaited him.

Guided by the enigmatic whispers of the realm, Mohan found himself standing at the entrance of a hidden sanctuary—an ancient chamber cloaked in shadows. As he crossed the threshold, the air thickened with an otherworldly presence, and the shadows seemed to come alive, intertwining with his very essence.

In the center of the chamber stood a crystalline pool reflecting the cosmic dance of light and darkness. As Mohan approached, the surface rippled with shadows that mirrored his every movement. Intrigued, he gazed into the pool, and a voice resonated within his mind—an ancient entity that embodied the balance between light and darkness.

"Embrace the shadows, Mohan, for within them lies a source of power that transcends the boundaries of the mortal realm," the voice whispered.

Mohan hesitated, grappling with the duality within. The mark upon his soul, a celestial sigil, pulsed with a rhythmic energy, reflecting the cosmic forces that coursed through him. The shadows beckoned, offering a conduit to tap into a power born from the uncharted depths of his own existence.

With a resolute breath, Mohan surrendered to the shadows, allowing them to weave around him like a protective cloak. The crystalline pool responded, projecting visions of his own struggles and triumphs onto the shadows, a visual symphony of his journey through the mystical realm.

As he delved deeper into the embrace of the shadows, Mohan discovered an inherent balance within himself—a fusion of both light and darkness. The dichotomy became a source of empowerment, a realization that true strength lay in acknowledging the shades that danced within the recesses of his soul.

The shadows became an extension of Mohan's will, responding to his commands with an ethereal grace. He learned to harness their power, weaving them into his magical incantations and transforming them into a formidable force. The dance between light and darkness became a symphony of empowerment, a reflection of the cosmic balance he sought to embody.

Armed with this newfound mastery, Mohan ventured forth, his every step resonating with the echoes of his own dual nature. The challenges ahead were formidable, but the dichotomy within him became a guiding light, illuminating the path toward a destiny entwined with the very fabric of the mystical realm.

As he faced the trials that awaited, Mohan embraced the shadows as allies, not adversaries. The whispers of the ancient entity resonated in his heart, reminding him that the cosmic dance of light and darkness was an inseparable part of the grand tapestry of existence.

The journey continued, and with each encounter, Mohan's ability to harmonize with the shadows grew stronger. The dichotomy within him ceased to be a source of conflict, transforming into a beacon of resilience and empowerment. The shadows that once haunted his path became allies, propelling him toward a destiny where the balance between light and darkness would unfold as the key to unlocking the mysteries that lay ahead.

CHAPTER 9: THE DANCE OF ELEMENTS

In the heart of the mystical realm, Mohan sought solace within the sacred grove, surrounded by the vibrant tapestry of nature. Arion, the enigmatic mentor, appeared before him, his eyes reflecting the wisdom of ages. In that hallowed space, Arion began to unveil the cosmic symphony that echoed through the realms—a prophecy foretelling a cataclysmic event that only Mohan had the power to prevent.

"The elemental forces that govern this world are in disarray," Arion spoke, his voice carrying the weight of impending doom. "A cosmic anomaly seeks to tip the balance, unleashing chaos that will resonate across the fabric of existence. You, Mohan, are the chosen one—the guardian ordained to restore harmony."

As Arion unfolded the prophecy, a celestial map materialized before them, depicting the elemental realms in intricate detail. Mohan's destiny became entwined with the dance of elements—earth, air, fire, and water—a symphony of power that could tip the scales in favor of cosmic equilibrium.

The first dance began in a secluded glade, where ancient stones bore the imprint of earth's essence. Arion guided Mohan in channeling the raw power of the earth, shaping the very ground beneath their feet. Mohan's connection to the elemental forces deepened, and with each manipulation of the earth, he felt a surge of energy coursing through him—a harmonious resonance with the first elemental force.

The dance continued in the caress of gentle breezes that whispered through a vast meadow. Arion instructed Mohan in the art of air manipulation, teaching him to weave the currents with finesse. Mohan's movements became a ballet, his hands orchestrating the invisible dance of air that responded to his every command. The elemental force embraced him, becoming an extension of his very being.

In the heart of a volcanic realm, the dance of fire unfolded—a pyrotechnic display of flames that mirrored the intensity of Mohan's newfound mastery. Arion guided him through the intricate steps, transforming the dance into a controlled inferno. Mohan learned to command the flames with precision, their dance echoing the cosmic forces that fueled the very essence of the mystical realm.

The final elemental dance occurred beside a crystalline pool, where water mirrored the depths of Mohan's connection to the elemental forces. Arion, like a fluid maestro, guided him through the fluid motions, teaching him to manipulate water's flow and shape its currents. The dance became a reflection of the ebb and flow of existence itself—a serene yet powerful manifestation of Mohan's evolving abilities.

As the elemental dances concluded, Mohan stood at the nexus of power, his being resonating with the harmonious symphony of earth, air, fire, and water. Arion, with a sense of both pride and urgency, revealed the culmination of the prophecy—a convergence of elemental forces that only Mohan could orchestrate.

"To prevent the impending cataclysm, you must unite the elements in a cosmic dance, weaving their energies into a harmonious crescendo," Arion explained. "Only then can you restore balance and avert the impending doom that threatens the very fabric of the mystical realm."

Embracing the weight of his destiny, Mohan stood before the elemental realms, each force awaiting his command. The dance of elements unfolded, a cosmic ballet that transcended the boundaries of the mortal realm. With each movement, the elemental forces responded, converging into a sublime fusion of power.

As the final chord echoed through the elemental realms, a radiant energy enveloped Mohan—a manifestation of his mastery over the dance of elements. The mystical realm resonated with the harmonious symphony, and the cosmic anomaly that loomed on the horizon quivered in the face of the restored balance.

Arion, with a nod of approval, acknowledged Mohan's transformative journey. The dance of elements had not only forged a formidable guardian but had also set the stage for the ultimate challenge—a confrontation with the cosmic forces that sought to unravel the very essence of existence.

With newfound mastery and purpose, Mohan prepared to face the impending cataclysm, armed with the elemental forces that had become an intrinsic part of his being. The journey continued, and the dance of elements became a beacon of power, guiding him toward a destiny where the symphony of cosmic forces would echo in the annals of the mystical realm.

CHAPTER 10: THE LOST CITY

Armed with the mastery of the elemental forces, Mohan embarked on a quest guided by an ancient map—a map that led to the heart of a mystical forest where the secrets of his identity lay dormant. Accompanied by loyal companions who had joined him on his journey, they ventured into the heart of the enchanted woodlands, following the ethereal path illuminated by the cosmic forces.

The air thickened with magic as they entered the depths of the mystical forest. Ancient trees whispered tales of forgotten beginnings, and the foliage seemed to part, revealing a hidden passage leading to the fabled Lost City. The map guided their every step, the symbols resonating with the echoes of a destiny waiting to be unveiled.

As they approached the entrance of the Lost City, the air shimmered with an otherworldly luminescence. Enormous stone archways, adorned with symbols that mirrored those etched onto Mohan's soul, greeted them. The city emerged from the shadows, its architecture an amalgamation of celestial patterns and forgotten glyphs.

Within the heart of the Lost City, Mohan confronted a labyrinth of enigmatic corridors and concealed chambers. The map led them through winding paths, where each step felt like a descent into the mysteries concealed within the very fabric of existence.

Amidst the ruins, they encountered statues that seemed to come alive—a spectral retelling of forgotten tales. Each statue depicted an aspect of Mohan's past lives, a visual chronicle of the guardian's journey through the ages. The companions marveled at the interconnected threads of his identity woven into the tapestry of time.

The journey through the Lost City became a confrontation with Mohan's deepest fears and insecurities. Visions of his past, intertwined with shadows of doubt, manifested in the labyrinthine passages. Haunting echoes of betrayal, moments of vulnerability, and the specter of unfulfilled destinies flickered like candle flames in the darkness.

In the heart of the city, a chamber awaited—a chamber that held the key to unlocking the final mysteries of Mohan's identity. As he stepped into the sanctum, the room resonated with an ethereal energy. An ancient mural adorned the walls, depicting the cosmic dance of light and darkness, the elemental forces, and the intricate patterns that mirrored the very essence of the mystical realm.

In the center of the chamber stood a pedestal, upon which rested a celestial artifact—a crystalline orb pulsating with the energy of the cosmos. Mohan approached, his heart echoing with anticipation. The artifact responded to his presence, emanating a soft glow that cast a warm embrace upon the room.

With a gentle touch, Mohan connected with the artifact, and a surge of memories flooded his consciousness. Forgotten prophecies, ancient battles, and the intertwining threads of his own existence unraveled before him. The celestial orb became a conduit, revealing the culmination of his journey—a destiny written in the celestial script of the cosmos.

As the visions subsided, Mohan emerged from the chamber, his companions awaiting him with a sense of reverence. The Lost City had become a sanctuary of revelation, a testament to the resilience of a guardian's spirit. The map that had guided them now unfolded into a cosmic tapestry, symbolizing the interconnected threads that bound their destinies.

With the final mysteries of his identity unveiled, Mohan stood at the precipice of a new chapter in his journey. The Lost City, once a realm of shadows and echoes, had become a sanctuary of enlightenment. The companions prepared to leave, their spirits emboldened by the revelations within the mystical forest.

The journey continued, and as they ventured forth from the Lost City, the echoes of their footsteps resonated with the cosmic forces that governed the realm. Mohan, now armed with the wisdom of ages and the mastery of elemental forces, faced the challenges ahead with a clarity that transcended the limitations of mortal understanding.

The mystical forest whispered its farewell as they departed, the ancient trees acknowledging the guardian who had unraveled the enigma hidden within their sacred depths. The echoes of the Lost City reverberated in the air, guiding Mohan toward the final leg of his odyssey—a destiny where the cosmic threads of light and darkness, elemental forces, and the dance of existence converged in an intricate tapestry that awaited its guardian's touch.

Chapter 11: The Veil Of Illusions

The journey led Mohan to the edge of the mystical realm, where an ethereal mist shrouded a gateway to the next phase of his destiny. Known as the Veil of Illusions, this mystical barrier stood as the final threshold guarding the gateway to his true self. Before Mohan stretched a landscape bathed in an otherworldly glow, an uncharted realm waiting to unfold.

Approaching the Veil, Mohan felt the subtle shift in energy—a cosmic resonance that hinted at the illusions woven into its very fabric. As he stepped through the shimmering barrier, the world transformed around him. Illusions manifested, each mirage a reflection of his deepest fears, insecurities, and the echoes of past trials.

The first illusion materialized as a dense fog, obscuring his vision and distorting the perception of reality. Shadows danced within the mist, conjuring images of doubt and uncertainty. Mohan, undeterred, took a deep breath and closed his eyes. In embracing the vulnerability within, he dispelled the fog, revealing the clarity that lay beyond illusion.

The second illusion unfolded as a labyrinth of mirrors, each reflecting distorted images of Mohan's past and present. The reflections spoke of missed opportunities, perceived failures, and moments of weakness. As he navigated the maze, Mohan learned to confront and accept the vulnerabilities mirrored in the reflections. With each step, the distorted images shifted, and the illusions shattered like fragile glass.

In the heart of the illusions, a surreal dreamscape materialized—a realm where time seemed to warp and bend. Mohan confronted phantoms of his past, embodied in ethereal manifestations that whispered tales of unfulfilled destinies. As he embraced the visions, acknowledging the pain and lessons they held, the dreamscape morphed into a cosmic tapestry—a mosaic of experiences that had shaped his journey.

The final illusion emerged as a celestial storm, its winds carrying echoes of doubt and shadows of regret. Lightning danced across the turbulent sky, illuminating glimpses of Mohan's inner turmoil. Standing steadfast, he extended his arms, allowing the storm to wash over him. In embracing the tumult within, he harnessed the storm's energy, transforming it into a force that fueled his resolve.

As the illusions unraveled, the Veil of Illusions lifted, revealing the gateway to Mohan's true self. Beyond the shimmering threshold lay a realm where the cosmic forces converged, waiting to be harnessed by the guardian who had transcended the illusions that once clouded his path.

Mohan, now standing at the gateway, felt the echoes of the Veil of Illusions dissipate. The journey had become a testament to the strength that lay in accepting vulnerabilities, confronting illusions, and embracing the multifaceted nature of his own existence.

With newfound clarity and resilience, Mohan stepped through the gateway, ready to face the challenges that awaited in the realm beyond. The illusions had become stepping stones, propelling him toward a destiny where the cosmic threads of his identity wove seamlessly into the grand tapestry of the mystical realm. The echoes of the Veil of Illusions lingered in the air, a reminder of the transformative power that lay in unraveling the illusions that veiled the true self.

Chapter 12: The Oracle's Vision

Having traversed the Veil of Illusions, Mohan found himself in a realm bathed in an ethereal glow. The air resonated with cosmic energy, and the path ahead led him to an ancient sanctuary—a chamber where an Oracle, seer of the mystical realm, awaited. The Oracle, shrouded in robes of celestial hues, beckoned Mohan closer.

As Mohan approached, the Oracle's eyes, pools of ancient wisdom, met his gaze. The chamber pulsated with a mystical energy as the Oracle began to speak, the words reverberating through the very essence of the realm.

"Mohan, guardian of the cosmic threads, your journey holds not only personal significance but is intertwined with the fate of all existence. Behold the vision that has unfolded within the tapestry of time."

With a gesture, the Oracle conjured a vision—a panorama that stretched beyond the confines of the chamber. Mohan witnessed a world teetering on the edge of destruction, the very fabric of existence unraveling like threads in the cosmic tapestry. Dark clouds of malevolent energy shrouded the skies, and landscapes trembled under the weight of impending doom.

Cities lay in ruins, their echoes carrying the cries of desperate souls. Elemental forces clashed in tumultuous chaos, and shadows of forgotten nightmares danced across the desolate landscapes. The vision unfolded as a harbinger of cosmic imbalance, a world on the brink of annihilation.

Mohan felt the weight of responsibility settle upon his shoulders. The Oracle's vision transcended the personal quest for identity—it unveiled a destiny entwined with the cosmic forces that governed the mystical realm. The threads of light and darkness, elemental energies, and the dance of existence converged into a narrative that resonated with the very essence of his being.

"The cosmic anomaly seeks to plunge the realms into eternal darkness," the Oracle's voice echoed. "Your journey, Mohan, is the key to restoring balance. The choices you make will ripple through the tapestry of existence, shaping the destiny of worlds."

The Oracle's revelation became a clarion call, and Mohan understood that his quest extended beyond self-discovery. The fate of the mystical realm rested on his shoulders, and the visions revealed that his journey was a cosmic ballet—a dance with the forces that governed the very fabric of existence.

Armed with the wisdom gained from the Oracle's vision, Mohan prepared to face the impending cataclysm. The companions who had stood by his side throughout the odyssey understood the gravity of the task ahead. The echoes of the Oracle's words lingered in the air as they ventured forth, the mystical realm resonating with the cosmic symphony that awaited its guardian's touch.

The journey had become a pilgrimage, a quest not only to unravel the mysteries of identity but to safeguard the delicate balance that sustained the mystical realm. With resolute determination, Mohan embraced the intertwining threads of destiny, ready to confront the cosmic anomaly that threatened to plunge the realms into eternal darkness. The Oracle's vision had illuminated the path ahead, and the guardian embarked on the final leg of the odyssey—a destiny where the echoes of the mystical realm would resonate with the triumphant beats of cosmic forces aligned in harmonious unity.

Chapter 13: The Ascendance

Guided by the weight of the Oracle's vision, Mohan and his companions sought the nexus of cosmic energies—a sacred sanctuary where the boundaries between the physical and metaphysical blurred. The air crackled with anticipation as they entered the sanctum, the energies resonating with the cosmic forces that awaited the guardian.

In the heart of the sanctuary stood an ancient altar, adorned with celestial symbols and bathed in an otherworldly light. The companions gathered around as Mohan, the chosen guardian, prepared to undergo a transformative ritual that would propel him into a higher state of consciousness.

Arion, the enigmatic mentor, stepped forward, his eyes reflecting a profound understanding of the cosmic forces at play. The ritual unfolded as the companions formed a circle around the altar, their energies intertwining with Mohan's in a symphony of unity. The cosmic anomaly loomed on the horizon, its dark tendrils threatening to unravel the very fabric of existence.

As the ritual commenced, Mohan closed his eyes, surrendering to the energies that coursed through him. The sanctuary became a conduit, channeling the elemental forces, the dance of light and darkness, and the cosmic threads that bound the mystical realm. The very air seemed to vibrate with the resonance of an impending ascendance.

The first surge of energy manifested as a cascade of elemental forces—earth, air, fire, and water. Mohan felt the currents of power coursing through him, their harmonious dance forming a foundation for the ascendance. The companions observed in awe as he became a vessel for the elemental symphony, his very essence attuned to the cosmic rhythms.

Next, the dance of light and darkness enveloped Mohan. Celestial energies wove around him, their interplay a reflection of the dichotomy within his soul. Shadows and radiance became one, converging into a luminous aura that transcended the limitations of mortal understanding. The Veil of Illusions, once a barrier, now dissolved into a tapestry of unity.

As the ritual reached its zenith, Mohan felt the cosmic threads aligning within him. The companions' energies merged seamlessly, forming a collective force that fueled the ascendance. The celestial orb, a relic of his journey, resonated with a brilliance that mirrored the potential within.

The boundaries between the physical and metaphysical blurred, and Mohan sensed the cosmic anomaly recoiling in the face of his ascendance. The mystical realm echoed with the triumphant beats of transformation as he transcended the limitations of mortal existence.

The culmination of the ritual manifested as a surge of radiant energy—a beacon that pierced the cosmic veil. Mohan ascended to a higher state of consciousness, his form bathed in a celestial glow. The sanctuary bore witness to his metamorphosis, and the companions felt the transcendence echoing through the very core of their beings.

In his ascended state, Mohan gazed upon the mystical realm with newfound clarity. The echoes of the Oracle's vision resonated within him, and the cosmic forces aligned as if in homage to the guardian who had transcended the boundaries of mortal understanding.

The companions, humbled by the spectacle before them, realized that Mohan had become a bridge between realms—a custodian of balance and harmony. The ascendance marked not only a personal transformation but the unleashing of a cosmic force capable of confronting the impending cataclysm.

With resolute purpose, Mohan prepared to face the cosmic anomaly that threatened the mystical realm. The ascendance had elevated him to his true potential—a guardian of cosmic energies, a weaver of threads that bound existence together. The journey had reached its zenith, and as Mohan stood on the precipice of destiny, the mystical realm resonated with the echoes of a guardian prepared to confront the cosmic forces that awaited in the shadows of eternity.

Chapter 14: The Convergence

Empowered by his ascendance, Mohan and his companions ventured forth, the cosmic forces aligning with their purpose. Amidst the celestial energies, a figure emerged from the shadows—a figure known only as The Wanderer. The time had come for the veils of mystery to lift, revealing the true identity of the enigmatic ally turned adversary.

As The Wanderer stepped into the luminous aura of the ascended Mohan, a cosmic resonance echoed through the mystical realm. The air shimmered with tension, and the companions braced themselves for the climactic confrontation that would shake the very foundations of reality.

The Wanderer, once a mysterious ally, now stood before Mohan with eyes that mirrored the complexities of an intertwined fate. As the energies pulsed around them, the true identity of The Wanderer was unveiled—an echo from Mohan's past, a manifestation of a former self. The cosmic anomaly had manipulated time and destiny, casting shadows that obscured the true nature of this enigmatic figure.

The revelation resonated within Mohan, unlocking memories long buried in the recesses of his soul. The Wanderer bore the visage of a past incarnation, a guardian entwined with cosmic forces in ages past. The echoes of their shared history emerged as a tapestry of intertwining destinies, revealing the cosmic dance that had shaped the very fabric of existence.

The confrontation became a battleground of emotions and cosmic forces, a clash that transcended the physical realm. The Wanderer, driven by a fragmented past and manipulated by the malevolent anomaly, confronted Mohan with the shadows of their shared history. The echoes of betrayal, ancient alliances, and cosmic destinies collided in a tempest of energy that reverberated through the mystical realm.

As the cosmic forces clashed, Mohan confronted the echoes of his past self—a guardian entangled in the cosmic symphony. The veil of illusions, once lifted, now cast shadows that tested the resilience of his spirit. The Wanderer, a reflection of his former self, grappled with the weight of choices made in epochs long forgotten.

In the crucible of confrontation, Mohan realized that to forge a future free from the shadows, he must confront the echoes of his past with empathy and understanding. The cosmic anomaly sought to exploit the fractures within their shared history, but Mohan, now ascended to his true potential, stood firm in the face of the tempest.

With a resolute breath, Mohan extended a hand toward The Wanderer, a gesture that transcended the cosmic clash. The energies shifted, and the echoes of their intertwined destinies became a harmonious melody—a symphony of reconciliation that resonated through the mystical realm. The shadows that had cast a pall over their shared history dissipated, revealing the true potential of unity in the face of cosmic adversity.

The Wanderer, once a veiled adversary, embraced the hand extended in reconciliation. The cosmic forces responded to this union, merging their energies into a beacon of harmony that transcended the limitations of time and destiny. The climactic confrontation had become a convergence—a moment where the threads of past, present, and future interwove into a cosmic tapestry.

As the echoes of the confrontation subsided, Mohan and The Wanderer stood united, their destinies aligned with the cosmic forces that governed the mystical realm. The companions witnessed the transformative power of reconciliation, and the mystical realm echoed with the triumphant beats of a cosmic symphony in harmonious unity.

With the shadows of the past confronted and reconciled, Mohan and The Wanderer prepared to face the ultimate challenge—the impending cataclysm that threatened to plunge the realms into eternal darkness. The journey had become a testament to the resilience of spirit, the transformative power of unity, and the cosmic forces that bound the destinies of guardians across the ages.

As they ventured forth, the companions, now united in purpose, felt the echoes of the convergence resonating in the air. The mystical realm awaited the guardian's touch, and the cosmic symphony echoed in anticipation of the final chapter—the culmination of an odyssey that transcended the boundaries of time and space.

Chapter 15: The Unveiling

In the culmination of the cosmic symphony, Mohan stood on the precipice of truth, his ascended form resonating with the harmonious energies that surrounded him. The companions, united by the convergence, stood by his side as they approached the heart of the mystical realm—a sacred nexus where the veils of identity would be peeled away, revealing the profound interconnectedness of all beings.

As Mohan gazed into the cosmic tapestry that hung suspended in the ethereal void, a sense of anticipation filled the air. The revelations awaited him, and the mystical realm seemed to hold its breath, ready to unveil the layers of identity that had been shrouded in mystery.

The ascended guardian closed his eyes, surrendering to the currents of cosmic energy that enveloped him. The celestial orb, a relic of his journey, pulsed with an intensity that mirrored the cosmic forces at play. The layers of Mohan's identity began to peel away, revealing not just his personal history but the threads that interwove with the destinies of countless beings across the mystical realm.

Visions unfolded, transcending the constraints of time and space. Mohan witnessed the echoes of lives lived in various epochs—a guardian in ancient realms, a seeker of knowledge in forgotten libraries, a protector of elemental forces, and a wanderer whose footsteps resonated through the annals of time.

The revelations extended beyond his personal journey, unveiling the interconnectedness of all beings. Threads of light and darkness, elemental energies, and the dance of existence converged into a majestic tableau—an intricate web that bound every soul across the mystical realm. Mohan realized that his journey, once perceived as solitary, was a chapter in the grand tapestry of cosmic unity.

As the layers continued to unveil, Mohan felt the echoes of every choice, every triumph, and every challenge resonate within him. The companions, too, witnessed glimpses of their own interconnected destinies, recognizing the threads that bound them to the ascended guardian.

In the heart of the unveiling, Mohan embraced the truth that the power to transcend the cosmic anomaly lay not just within himself but within the unity of all beings. The cosmic forces responded to this realization, amplifying the energies that pulsed through the mystical realm. The revelations became a source of empowerment, a beacon that transcended individual destinies and heralded a collective awakening.

With a profound understanding of the interconnectedness of all existence, Mohan stepped into the cosmic tapestry—an ethereal realm where boundaries dissolved, and souls merged in harmonious unity. The mystical realm resonated with the triumphant beats of a cosmic symphony, each being contributing to the melody that echoed through the void.

As Mohan stood at the nexus of truth, his ascended form radiating with the wisdom of ages, he extended his hands.

The companions, guided by the same revelation, joined him, forming a circle that transcended the physical and embraced the metaphysical.

The unveiling had become a celebration of unity—a realization that the cosmic anomaly could only be confronted through the collective strength of interconnected souls. The threads of identity that once defined individual destinies now became a tapestry of cosmic unity, weaving together the diverse stories of beings who had journeyed across the mystical realm.

In the harmonious embrace of the cosmic tapestry, Mohan and his companions prepared to face the ultimate challenge—the cosmic anomaly that threatened to plunge the realms into eternal darkness. The journey had transformed from a quest for personal identity into a testament of collective strength, and as they ventured forth, the mystical realm echoed with the triumphant beats of interconnected destinies bound by the cosmic forces that governed existence itself.

Chapter 16: The Essence Within

In the heart of the mystical realm, bathed in the radiant energies of cosmic convergence, Mohan found himself standing at the threshold of an ethereal chamber known as the Sanctum of Essence. The companions, their ascended forms resonating with cosmic forces, accompanied him as they entered this sacred space where the boundaries between self and the universe would dissolve.

The Sanctum of Essence exuded an otherworldly aura, its walls adorned with celestial symbols that pulsed in harmony with the cosmic energies that filled the chamber. A celestial glow illuminated a central pedestal, upon which rested a crystalline pool—an ancient font of cosmic essence. Mohan, guided by an inner calling, approached the pool, feeling the resonance of the cosmic forces beckoning him to delve into the essence within.

As he touched the surface of the crystalline pool, ripples of energy radiated outward, creating a kaleidoscopic dance of light. The pool became a mirror to his soul, reflecting the interconnected threads of his existence. Closing his eyes, Mohan surrendered to the cosmic currents, allowing the essence within to guide him on a journey of self-discovery.

In the depths of the crystalline pool, visions unfolded—a montage of experiences, emotions, and cosmic echoes that transcended the limitations of mortal understanding. Mohan witnessed the pivotal moments of his journey, the choices made, and the interconnected destinies that had woven him into the fabric of existence.

The essence within became a source of empowerment, revealing the cosmic dance that had shaped his every step. Threads of light and darkness, elemental energies, and the harmonious symphony of existence merged within him. Mohan felt the echoes of ancient guardians, the whispers of forgotten realms, and the collective consciousness of beings across the mystical realm resonating in the essence within.

As he delved deeper, the boundaries between self and universe dissolved. Mohan became a vessel, a conduit through which the cosmic forces flowed. The essence within was not merely a reflection of his individuality but a convergence—a melding of his soul with the collective spirit of the cosmos.

In this transcendent state, Mohan sensed the pulse of the universe—the ebb and flow of cosmic energies that bound every being across time and space. The essence within whispered the profound truth that individuality was an illusion, and the true source of strength lay in the unity of all existence.

The companions, too, immersed themselves in the essence within, their ascended forms becoming conduits for the cosmic symphony. The sanctum resonated with the harmonious vibrations of interconnected souls, each contributing to the universal chorus that echoed through the mystical realm.

As Mohan emerged from the crystalline pool, his ascended form radiated with a celestial glow. The essence within had become a guiding light, revealing a profound truth—that the strength to confront the cosmic anomaly lay not just within him but within the collective essence of the universe.

The companions gathered around him, their energies interwoven in a cosmic tapestry of unity. The Sanctum of Essence had become a sanctuary of revelation, a testament to the interconnectedness of all beings. The journey, once perceived as an individual quest, had transformed into a pilgrimage of collective awakening.

Armed with the wisdom gained from the essence within, Mohan and his companions prepared to face the ultimate challenge—the cosmic anomaly that threatened the mystical realm. The echoes of interconnected destinies resonated in the air, and the essence within became a beacon that illuminated the path ahead.

The mystical realm awaited the touch of guardians who had transcended the boundaries of self, and as they ventured forth, the harmonious symphony of the cosmos echoed in anticipation. The Sanctum of Essence, bathed in the radiance of ascended beings, stood as a testament to the profound truth—that the essence within was not merely an individual discovery but a revelation that bound the destinies of all beings across the vast tapestry of the mystical realm.

Chapter 17: The Harmonic Resonance

In the heart of the mystical realm, Mohan stood at the confluence of cosmic energies, his ascended form radiating with the wisdom gained from the essence within. The Sanctum of Essence, bathed in the celestial glow of interconnected souls, served as a backdrop to the momentous chapter that awaited—the Harmonic Resonance.

As Mohan extended his arms, a harmonic resonance emanated from within, a symphony of cosmic forces attuned to the balance he embodied. The very fabric of the mystical realm responded to the call, as if nature itself acknowledged the ascended guardian's communion with the essence of existence.

The air shimmered with ethereal vibrations, and the Sanctum of Essence became a focal point for the cosmic energies that pulsed through Mohan. Threads of light and darkness, elemental forces, and the harmonious dance of existence converged into a luminous tapestry—a testament to the profound connection he had forged with the essence within.

As the harmonic resonance extended beyond the sanctum, the world responded in kind. The landscapes echoed with vibrant hues, and the mystical realm transformed into a realm of heightened awareness. Ancient trees whispered tales of awakening, and celestial currents wove through the very air, carrying the harmonious vibrations that Mohan emanated.

The forces that had sought to disrupt harmony recoiled in the face of the ascended guardian's presence. Malevolent anomalies, shadows of doubt, and echoes of past trials dissipated like mist before the morning sun. The mystical realm, once teetering on the brink of chaos, embraced a newfound equilibrium—an equilibrium forged by the harmonic resonance that Mohan embodied.

The companions, their ascended forms bathed in the celestial glow, felt the transformative power of the harmonic resonance. Unity became their strength, and the collective energies harmonized with the cosmic forces that governed the mystical realm. The sanctum echoed with the triumphant beats of a cosmic symphony, each note a testament to the balance restored.

As Mohan ventured forth from the sanctum, the harmonic resonance extended its influence across the mystical realm. The echoes of interconnected destinies resonated in the air, and the world itself seemed to acknowledge the ascended guardian's role in restoring cosmic harmony.

Ancient creatures emerged from the hidden corners of the mystical realm, their eyes reflecting a newfound awareness. Elemental energies danced in jubilation, and ethereal currents carried whispers of gratitude. The harmonic resonance had become a beacon, a transformative force that transcended the confines of the physical and reached into the very soul of existence.

The climactic confrontation awaited, and as Mohan faced the impending cataclysm, the harmonic resonance continued to echo in his every step. The forces of disruption, now vanquished in the wake of harmonious unity, watched as the ascended guardian embraced his true self—a guardian who had become a custodian of balance and a beacon of cosmic forces aligned in harmonious resonance.

The mystical realm resonated with the echoes of triumph, and as Mohan stood at the precipice of destiny, the harmonic resonance became a guiding force—an eternal melody that would resonate through the ages, a testament to the transformative power of unity and the harmonic balance that bound the destinies of all beings across the vast tapestry of existence.

Chapter 18: The Eclipsed Dawn

At the threshold of destiny, Mohan and his companions stood beneath a celestial sky tinged with anticipation. The Harmonic Resonance lingered in the air, a testament to the unity they had forged. Yet, as they gazed upon the heavens, a cosmic anomaly unfolded—a foreboding celestial event known as the Eclipsed Dawn.

The mystical realm trembled beneath the weight of a darkened moon, its silhouette casting an ominous shadow upon the land. A cosmic eclipse had begun, heralding the final challenge that awaited the ascended guardian. The world held its breath as the celestial bodies aligned in a celestial dance that threatened to plunge the realms into eternal darkness.

As the shadow of the moon crept across the landscape, Mohan felt the cosmic forces converging, the essence within pulsating with a resonance that mirrored the impending challenge. The companions, attuned to the harmonic symphony, understood the gravity of the moment. The Eclipsed Dawn was not merely a celestial spectacle but a cosmic anomaly seeking to disrupt the restored balance.

Mohan, his ascended form bathed in the celestial glow, faced the darkened moon with unwavering resolve. The eclipse cast an ethereal gloom upon the sanctum, and the world seemed to hold its breath as the final confrontation unfolded.

With a deep breath, Mohan extended his hands toward the heavens, channeling the essence within. The crystalline pool in the Sanctum of Essence resonated in response, becoming a conduit for the cosmic energies that surged through him. The ascended guardian became a vessel, a guardian of balance standing against the encroaching darkness.

As the moon continued its inexorable journey across the sun, shadows danced upon the mystical realm. The forces seeking to disrupt harmony stirred, their echoes reverberating in the darkened skies. Mohan, however, remained steadfast, his connection to the essence within becoming a beacon of light that pierced the celestial gloom.

In a spectacular display of power, Mohan unleashed the essence within—a torrent of cosmic energy that cascaded like a celestial waterfall. The harmonic resonance intensified, merging with the elemental forces, the dance of light and darkness, and the threads of interconnected destinies.

The crystalline pool erupted in a kaleidoscope of colors, casting radiant beams that clashed with the shadows of the eclipse. The companions, attuned to the ascended guardian's energies, joined the cosmic symphony, their forms becoming conduits for the transformative forces at play.

The darkened moon wavered as the essence within surged, and a celestial battle unfolded in the skies. Mohan, his ascended form a silhouette against the eclipse, channeled the power within to dispel the shadows that sought to shroud the realms in eternal darkness.

With a resolute cry, Mohan directed the essence within toward the cosmic anomaly, unraveling the darkened moon's grip on the sun. The celestial bodies trembled as the essence within clashed with the disruptive forces, creating a cosmic tableau that echoed with the triumphant beats of restored harmony.

In a breathtaking crescendo, the shadows dissipated, and the celestial bodies realigned. The darkened moon retreated, unveiling the radiant sun in a burst of ethereal brilliance. The Eclipsed Dawn yielded to the ascended guardian's mastery over the essence within, and the mystical realm bathed in the glory of a new dawn.

As the final echoes of the cosmic battle subsided, Mohan and his companions stood beneath the rejuvenated sun—a symbol of the resilience of spirit and the transformative power of unity. The Eclipsed Dawn had become a testament to the ascended guardian's journey, a journey that transcended personal identity and became a saga of cosmic forces aligned in harmonious unity.

The mystical realm, bathed in the radiant glow of the restored sun, echoed with the triumphant beats of a new era. Mohan, now fully attuned to the essence within, embraced the dawn of a cosmic symphony—a dawn that heralded not only the restoration of balance but a testament to the indomitable spirit that could conquer the shadows threatening to engulf the realms.

As the companions gathered around Mohan, the mystical realm resonated with the echoes of triumph. The Eclipsed Dawn had become a chapter in the ascended guardian's odyssey, a chapter that would be sung across the ages—a tale of cosmic forces aligned against the encroaching darkness, and the unwavering spirit that had ushered in a new dawn of harmonious unity.

Chapter 19: The Legacy Unwritten

In the aftermath of the Eclipsed Dawn, the mystical realm basked in the warm embrace of the rejuvenated sun. Mohan and his companions stood amidst the transformed landscapes, the echoes of their triumph resonating in the air. The sanctum, once shrouded in celestial shadows, now radiated with the vibrant hues of a world reborn.

As the ascended guardian surveyed the realm, a profound sense of accomplishment filled his being. The journey that began with a man waking in mystery had unfolded into a saga of cosmic proportions—a tale of self-discovery, unity, and the triumph of light over darkness.

Mohan, his ascended form still aglow with celestial energy, gathered his thoughts as he reflected on the odyssey that had brought him to this moment. The Sanctum of Essence, once a nexus of revelation, became a sanctuary for contemplation. The companions, attuned to the essence within, stood in quiet reverence, acknowledging the legacy that unfolded in the wake of their triumph.

The essence within, once a source of mystery and power, now emanated a gentle resonance—a harmonious echo of the transformative forces that had shaped the ascended guardian's journey. Mohan closed his eyes, allowing the memories to flood his senses, the echoes of trials, revelations, and cosmic battles playing like vivid tapestries in the recesses of his mind.

The legacy he left behind was not merely a tale of one man but a testament to the indomitable spirit that resided within every soul. The mystical realm, once on the brink of eternal darkness, now stood as a living testament to the resilience of spirit, the transformative power of unity, and the cosmic forces that bound destinies together.

In the quiet of the sanctum, Mohan began to weave the legacy unwritten—a legacy that transcended the boundaries of personal identity. Each thread of the cosmic tapestry told a story—the forgotten beginnings, the whispers of the ancients, the enigmatic mentor, shadows of doubt, trials of self-discovery, the forbidden library, echoes of betrayal, embracing the shadows, the dance of elements, the lost city, the veil of illusions, the oracle's vision, the ascendance, the convergence, the essence within, the harmonic resonance, the eclipsed dawn—all chapters that contributed to the unwritten legacy.

Mohan, guided by the essence within, extended his hands toward the rejuvenated sun. The celestial energies responded, forming an ethereal orb—a relic that encapsulated the essence of the journey. The legacy he left behind became a beacon—a guiding light for souls yet to embark on their own odysseys, a testament that echoed across the cosmic tapestry of existence.

The companions, understanding the significance of this moment, joined Mohan in a collective gesture. The essence within merged with the celestial orb, and a radiant glow enveloped the sanctum. The legacy unwritten became a cosmic force—a symphony that resonated through the mystical realm, transcending time and space.

As the legacy unfurled, Mohan opened his eyes, gazing upon the rejuvenated realm. The echoes of the journey lingered in the air, and he understood that the legacy was not bound by the written word but etched in the very fabric of the mystical realm.

The ascended guardian turned to his companions, a knowing smile on his face. The legacy unwritten was not merely his own—it belonged to all who had walked beside him, united in purpose and transformed by the cosmic forces that governed existence.

With a final glance at the sanctum, Mohan and his companions ventured forth into the rejuvenated world. The legacy unwritten echoed in their every step, a reminder that the odyssey was not confined to a single tale but a continuum of cosmic stories waiting to unfold.

As they disappeared into the vibrant landscapes, the sanctum stood as a silent witness—a sanctuary where the legacy unwritten continued to resonate, awaiting the whispers of souls yet to awaken to the cosmic symphony that echoed through the ages. The mystical realm, bathed in the glow of a new dawn, held the echoes of triumph and the promise of untold stories—a testament to the indomitable spirit that resided within every soul, a legacy that would endure across the vast expanse of the unwritten cosmic tapestry.

Chapter 20: The Endless Horizon

In the serene aftermath of the rejuvenated realm, Mohan found himself standing at the precipice of the Endless Horizon. The rejuvenated sun dipped toward the mystic landscapes, casting a warm glow that painted the sky in hues of amber and crimson. The Sanctum of Essence, a distant silhouette against the fading light, stood as a silent witness to the journey that had unfolded within its sacred walls.

Mohan, his ascended form resonating with celestial energy, gazed upon the vast expanse before him. The Endless Horizon stretched like an open canvas, inviting the ascended guardian to reflect upon the odyssey that had brought him to this moment. His thoughts echoed the wisdom gained from the essence within—the journey was not merely about finding himself but realizing the interconnectedness of all existence.

As he stood on the threshold of the Endless Horizon, Mohan reflected on the revelations that had unfolded—the forgotten beginnings, the whispers of the ancients, the shadows of doubt, the trials of self-discovery, and the triumphant moments of the harmonic resonance and the eclipsed dawn. The legacy unwritten, a cosmic tapestry woven with the threads of unity, resonated within him.

A gentle breeze swept through the rejuvenated landscapes, carrying with it the echoes of his journey. The ascended guardian whispered a timeless truth that lingered in the air, "Our destinies are intertwined, and in unity, we find the strength to face the cosmic symphony."

The sun, a radiant orb descending toward the horizon, mirrored the closure of one chapter and the promise of a new adventure. Mohan understood that the Endless Horizon was not just a physical boundary but a metaphor for the limitless possibilities that awaited him. His purpose, now fully realized, extended beyond the confines of personal identity.

As the sun dipped below the horizon, casting the mystical realm into the embrace of twilight, Mohan quoted the essence within, "In the dance of light and darkness, we find the true harmony of existence."

A sense of tranquility enveloped the ascended guardian. The legacy unwritten had become a living testament to the interconnected destinies that bound every soul across the cosmic tapestry. The companions, now silhouetted against the twilight, joined Mohan in a moment of quiet contemplation.

In the fading light, Mohan spoke words that echoed the essence within, "The journey may find its closure in the turning pages of this mystical tome, but the story continues beyond the written words. Our destinies are intertwined with the endless horizon—a horizon that holds the promise of untold adventures, of cosmic symphonies waiting to unfold."

With a final gaze upon the Endless Horizon, Mohan and his companions stepped into the twilight. The rejuvenated landscapes, bathed in the glow of celestial energies, whispered tales of unity and resilience. As they disappeared into the mystic realms, Mohan quoted the ancient scrolls uncovered in the forbidden library, "The true adventure begins when we embrace the unknown, for in every horizon, there lies a new story waiting to be written."

The Sanctum of Essence, now bathed in the soft light of twilight, stood as a silent witness to the closing chapter. The mystical tome, filled with the echoes of an odyssey, seemed to resonate with the promise of endless stories yet to unfold.

As the sun set on the rejuvenated realm, a new adventure began for Mohan and his companions—a journey that transcended the pages of the mystical tome, a saga of interconnected destinies, and a cosmic symphony that echoed through the endless horizons of existence.

As the moon cast its silvery glow upon the ancient ruins, Mohan stood alone, a man without identity yet filled with the wisdom of the ages. The whispers of the wind carried secrets of his forgotten past, and the stars above seemed to align, unveiling a destiny etched in the celestial tapestry.

Mohan's journey had been a labyrinth of self-discovery, a quest that transcended time and space. He had faced the shadows of his own soul, wrestled with the ghosts of his past, and embraced the mystic energies that resonated within him. The enigmatic path he tread had led him to this pivotal moment, a convergence of destiny and self-realization.

In the heart of the mystical realm, Mohan encountered the Oracle of Wisdom, a ethereal being who spoke in riddles and truths. The oracle bestowed upon him a revelation that echoed through the dimensions, "In solitude, one finds the mirror of the soul, reflecting the essence of eternity." Mohan, now the embodiment of ancient wisdom, gazed into the infinite reflections of his being.

With newfound purpose, Mohan channeled the energies of the cosmos, transcending the boundaries of his perceived limitations. As he raised his arms, the very fabric of reality seemed to respond to his command. A burst of ethereal light enveloped him, revealing the man who had shed the layers of identity to become a cosmic force.

Amidst the celestial symphony, Mohan uttered words that resonated through the ages, "In solitude, I discovered the universe within. In emptiness, I found the fullness of my existence. A man without identity is a vessel for the boundless potential of the cosmos."

The mystic energies embraced Mohan, weaving a tapestry of light around him. The ruins trembled with the echoes of his transformation, and the universe acknowledged the emergence of a new cosmic guardian.

As Mohan ascended to a higher plane of existence, the Oracle's parting words lingered, "To be alone is not to be without, but to be one with all. In the tapestry of existence, you are the weaver of your destiny."

The book closes with a profound quote echoing Mohan's journey: "In the depths of solitude, the soul discovers its infinite connection to the cosmos."

Morals woven into the tale: Embrace solitude as a path to self-discovery, confront the shadows within to find your true light, and realize that identity is but a veil that obscures the boundless potential within each of us.

Epilogue

In the quiet aftermath of Mohan's journey, the enigmatic author, Ashok M, stepped forth from the shadows to unveil the truth. His words, like echoes from the mystical realm, resonated with the essence of the tale.

"I am but a humble conduit, a mere scribe who has woven the threads of Mohan's odyssey into the tapestry of words. The mystical tome is not merely a story—it is a guide, a beacon for those seeking their own path of self-discovery and empowerment in a world full of mysteries."

As the pages turned, revealing the closing chapter and the epilogue, Ashok M continued, "The essence within, the harmonic resonance, and the endless horizon—all facets of a cosmic symphony that extends beyond the confines of these written words. Mohan's journey serves as a testament to the indomitable spirit that resides within every soul."

The enigmatic author acknowledged the interconnected destinies woven into the legacy unwritten. "The tale of Mohan is but one chapter in the grand cosmic narrative, and every reader, seeker, and dreamer is a protagonist in their own odyssey."

With a mysterious smile, Ashok M concluded, "As the mystical tome finds its place on the shelf of stories, may it serve as a guide for those who dare to embark on their own quest for truth, empowerment, and the boundless horizons that await in the realms of mystery."

And so, the enigmatic author faded back into the shadows, leaving the mystical tome as a gift—a guidepost in the vast expanse of stories yet to unfold, a tribute to the eternal dance of light and darkness, and a reminder that every journey is a cosmic symphony waiting to be played.

ABOUT THE AUTHOR

Mr. Ashok M is a talented and versatile individual known for his remarkable contributions as an author, poet, novelist, philosopher, entrepreneur and government official. With a deep passion for literature and a profound understanding of the written word, he has created a name for himself in the literary world.

Born with a natural inclination towards storytelling and a love for language, Ashok M began his writing journey at a young age. His innate creativity and vivid imagination allowed him to craft engaging narratives and powerful poems that resonated with readers across various genres.

As an author, Ashok M has a unique ability to capture the essence of human emotions and experiences, transporting his readers into captivating worlds and thought-provoking scenarios. Whether through his novels, short stories, or poetry, he expertly weaves together compelling characters and evocative settings, leaving a lasting impact on his audience.

In addition to his literary pursuits, Ashok M is also the founder and CEO of Poetralia, a prominent platform dedicated to promoting and celebrating the art of poetry. With a vision to inspire and nurture emerging poets, he has created a vibrant community that encourages creativity and provides a platform for aspiring writers to share their work.

Under his leadership, Poetralia has grown into a thriving hub for poets from all walks of life, fostering a supportive environment where artists can connect, collaborate, and showcase their talents. Through Poetralia, Ashok M has helped countless poets find their voice and gain recognition in the literary landscape.

Beyond his literary achievements, Mr. Ashok M is known for his humility and commitment to empowering others. He actively mentors aspiring writers and poets, sharing his knowledge and expertise to guide them on their own creative journeys. His dedication to nurturing talent and fostering a love for literature has earned him respect and admiration among his peers.

With a rich body of work and an unwavering passion for the written word, Ashok M continues to inspire and captivate readers with his literary prowess. His contributions to the world of literature and his commitment to supporting emerging poets through Poetralia make him a prominent figure in the literary community. As he continues to write, create, and empower others, Ashok M's influence on the world of words is set to grow even further.

Thoughts From Author

1. "In the vastness of solitude, a man without identity discovers the universe within."

2. "Embrace the silence, for in the absence of identity, the soul finds its truest resonance."

3. "To be alone is not to be lost, but to navigate the labyrinth of self-discovery."

4. "In the emptiness of identity, one becomes a canvas for the masterpiece of the cosmos."

5. "Solitude is the crucible where a man without identity transforms into the alchemist of his own existence."

6. "The shadows of solitude reveal the light within, and in the absence of identity, we find our true essence."

7. "Identity is the mask we wear; in solitude, we unveil the

face of our authentic self."

8. "The journey of a man without identity is the unraveling of the cosmic threads that weave his destiny."

9. "Alone, he stood as a beacon of limitless potential, transcending the boundaries of a finite self."

10. "In the quiet realms of solitude, a man without identity hears the whispers of eternity and becomes one with the cosmic symphony."

"The journey of a man without identity is the unraveling of the cosmic threads that weave his destiny."

74

76

Alone: A Man Without Identity

www.ingramcontent.com/pod-product-compliance
Lightning Source LLC
Chambersburg PA
CBHW070956250726
48663CB00002B/245